ISABELLA MOTADINYANE
complete poems

ISABELLA MOTADINYANE
complete poems

ISBN: 978-0-9870282-7-3
ebook ISBN: 978-1-928476-23-8

Deep South
contact@deepsouth.co.za
www.deepsouth.co.za

Distributed in South Africa by
University of KwaZulu-Natal Press
www.ukznpress.co.za

Distributed worldwide by
African Books Collective
PO Box 721, Oxford, OX1 9EN, UK
www.africanbookscollective.com/publishers/deep-south

Deep South acknowledges the financial assistance of
the National Arts Council for the production of this book

NATIONAL ARTS COUNCIL
OF SOUTH AFRICA

Sesotho translations by Lesego Rampolokeng

Cover design: Liz Gowans and Robert Berold
Text design and layout: Liz Gowans
Cover photograph: Michael Jaspan

Publisher's note

Isabella Motadinyane, who died in 2003 aged 40, had a style of writing and performing that was entirely her own. On the page her poems were intense, funny and painful, while her onstage delivery, whether speech or song, was electrifying in its vitality and timing. Her elliptical and associative poems mixed languages, crossed rural and urban cultures.

Isabella was an active member of the Botsotso Jesters poetry performance group, in fact the group's name came from one of her poems. Her collected work – just over 30 poems – was published as *Bella* in 2007 by Botsotso Publishing. The book included touching tributes by other Botsotso members which are reprinted in this edition.

Why the need to republish? Mainly because *Bella* had a full page drawing opposite every poem, and I felt that the drawings overwhelmed the poems. A few years ago I asked the Botsotso people if I could publish a new edition without the drawings, and they agreed. Lesego Rampolokeng made new translations of the six Sesotho poems and the Sesotho phrases scattered in other poems.

I hope this new edition of Isabella's collected work will contribute to keeping her spirit and her poetry alive.

Robert Berold, Deep South

Isabella Motadinyane publications:
We Jive Like This (Botsoto Publishing, 1996)
Dirty Washing (Botsotso Publishing, 1999)
Bella (collected poems from the above two books, Botsotso Publishing, 2003)

Recorded performances:
Jikeleza Train (VHS video from 1998 Performance Festival, ISEA, 1999)
Purple Light Mirror in the Mud (CD Botsotso Jesters, 2001)
Poetry 99 (DVD + book from 1999 Performance Festival, Deep South, 2013)

Contents

TRIBUTES

Shadows and things

Moving shadows thicken on walls
voices become fluffy
to listening ears
but through mental errors
i stitched my speech
to set my back free
'just to let go'
an angel hanging from a thread
then heavy voices dropped from lollipops
shadows peeling off walls
i took a few strides to the bathroom
there i met a familiar stranger in the mirror
don't remember the self any more
only voices calling after me
on a full moon, under moving shadows
i left my mark on the floor

You pulled an elastic

You pulled an elastic
down my legs
i looked into your eyes
and said words
you wanted to hear

with the reflection of the moon on your face
tickling pores of awareness in me
i spread my sea wings apart
for you to come in

In a jet

in a jet
ka sega phefo
to pick-pay
scissor cut right pants
springbok security checks
united with Joshua
the door keeper
Metropolitan gave me a tusk
for recording songs i sing
Van Jivan
via people's library
Musiekie Africa
bringing windy-brows
after a professional score
at the Yard of Ale
on my black and white
portable television i saw
Market Laboratory destroy
New Coin Staffriders

I cut the wind

Walking on ice

When the house
thronged
with people
silence
aware of his presence
i read his words
from the thin
of his lips
"this poem is 'bout to start"
walking on ice
he had a mind
to let go
but watched time
the unblinking eye
watched SA
through a telescope
saw a long walk to freedom
allowed one visit a month
a long walk to freedom
with a handful of names
enough to destroy a government
saw an old man sitting on the rim of his chair
taking off his jacket
giving it to the young
walking on ice
a woman from India
jumped on stage
bit his ear
"walk off you screw
get off the scope
you poison the minds of our people"
walking on ice
he is the face

of satisfied laughter
he bleached the night
he held the sun high
he knew the sky
will never fall
when walking on ice

Hungry violent boys crack

Hungry violent boys crack
a blue movie sound track
weaving seeds of sin pact
counting one two three
they keep their dreams intact
against cracked walls of fate
one foot tripped off in a dream
another bites the stream
dreams that felt the strain
from his tinted brain kicking
his mental blackout tricks
searching their backs for coin stacks
it is cold down there
they chant a slogan for warmth
release all prisoners
praise poets of the people
for a comfortable position
thin circles of fate stretched out

I was cooking

I was cooking in the kitchen
he sat there folding arms
my body carrying his eyes around
he was actually ogling me
huffing sounds suddenly emerged from behind
i slowly turned round fed up
knowing how sharp my tongue can be
he coaxed my smile
to melt the mask from my face
i grinned and said hi
he winked an eye and sheepishly asked
who is it that you are seeing lately
ag man
did he have possessions before
                                i thought aloud

Welcome to reality

Welcome to reality
in white shorts
and maroon top
her footsteps calculated
click-clock
from the entrance
watching her sharp edges
collect loose ends

welcome with open arms
all over her body
he longed to feel
touch with his soul
talk to his secretary bird
a magnet on the loose
set their bodies on fire
burning lips pink
chapped tits wet
washed memories of
long time no see

giving way to reality
they multiplied
a blanket on the grass
by a shadow under the sun
she engulfed his third leg
friction propelling warning shots
on their faces
i am am coming
i am also coming I am ...

Welcome to reality

Slow motion brain slide

Slow motion brain slide
on a cold prison cell floor
money mongers suffering
scalp arthritis
reveal shadows of greed
anticipating to step onto the gravy train
where men bring brains to think
stale memories of
kangaroo court

She walked a painful lane home

She walked a painful lane home
wiping tears of change
from her soiled body
but told no one about those fakes

Now her poison intake
lays skin on her bones
perspires with naked truth

Reading her medical record
as three little words
holding back the years

My bruised soul

My bruised soul
colour my face pale
identity gradually fading
trying to stretch
wrinkle lines straight
On my face
ounces and pounds
drop and drain energy
off my shoulders weak
my night shrieks
shock the neighbours
"this is weird
is she eaten up by rooi miere?"   *red ants*
they cry
feeling my pain
my tears
Pulling a sinking boat
created me pains

Dirty washing smells

Paralysing my nostrils
back ache strokes
pushing me over the edge of
thato ya hao e etsiwe lefatsheng   *your will be done on earth*

Wash their antique's stooled laundry
          that's good my love
Scrub the antique's stools funnel clean
          that's excellent my love

An antique has visited the west
I heard it in my sleep
          you must pack your bags and go
          immediately after tears
          your job is done now

An award shoved up my arse hole
lost my campaign for a seat
in home affairs

So i packed my humble words
one by one
pulled my shadows together
and closed the door behind me

How far from here
i failed to answer bags
on my back
leaving memory off-cuts
for failed abortions to eat
and die a rotting death

Tie her up

Tie her up
Lock her in
bring the keys here
and go away
Said a limping man
with a walking stick

Beyond the grave

My name lands
beyond the grave
stripping down my being
the cry of my
flesh remnants
gripped by space
While the yester-me
rusts in the wilderness
fighting wild weather
pleading pleading
give me tonight - only tonight
but softly softly my name lands
beyond the grave
mispronounced
they stretch my next-of-kin's patience
but can't skin me pinker
beyond the grave
leaving me a narrow view
the blue sky
pouring soil on my chest
freezing my plea
give me tonight
my plea site-line begs
this grave
this cold weathered grave
just laid eyes on me
the verdict is simple
my skin
the colour of soil

Sink a shaft

Dark night babe
toss and turn
the clouds above
you make the sober go drunk
come in from the cold
warm you up
sink down our throat
the clouds above
mountains so high
sink babe sink
sink a shaft
move slowly down the mountain
down our throats
toss and turn babe
sink on me
all night
dark clouds above
you make the sober go drunk
sink babe sink
sink it smooth
sink a shaft

Touting taxi

Touting taxi
topsy
turvey
pep talk
from Zola
to Jozi
music background
loud and loud
pep talk
trace
toilet tissue
tracks
van bo
ke bona dibono   *I see buttocks*
ke sa bone   *without seeing*
beng ba tsona   *whose they are*
taxi
topsy turvey
pep talk
constant thuggery
criss cross
cross pollination
Christianity charged
short cut corner
Magomosha style   *tsotsi style*
corner
Market and Nugget
taxi topsy
turvey
pep talk
drinking beefeaters
eyes off
melting bazookas

meaty juice
ba harela jwala   *they guzzle alcohol*
eke ba kgaohile maoto   *as if their legs were cut off*
kwala molomo lovey   *shut your mouth lovey*
ke mametse   *I'm listening to*
touting taxi
topsy turvey
pep talk

Stella

Stella Stella
I've been to your home
I found your mama there
she said
you left long ago

I saw tears in her eyes
and I knew
it was real
Stella come home
to me
Stella Stella
there is no life without you
our kids are missing you
you know I love you so
come back
Stella Stella

Stella please come home
I've been to your home
I found your mama there
she said
you left long ago
left her sick
and hungry ...

Television

In my dreams
tell a vision
you sitting on the loo
red lips
chewing gums
smoking cigarettes
between your fingers
your eyes see
a central line
in a vision
of my dreams
cats can pass

One leg in

One leg in
another leg out
tight me up
strongly sewn
visible mending
back pocket trademark
silver buttons attached
not woven once
twice or thrice
die is mos botsotsos   *(skin-tight denim jeans)*
back pocket
front pocket
nog 'n maal talk to me
die is mos botsotsos
pull high
stretch on a high way
ons pedestry moet doves   *we travel with doves*
no attention to whistlers my weebit
no hearing sweet nothings
strongly sewn
die is mos botsotsos

White lace

White lace
darkens voices
your scarface
calls
at a distance
Shwele Baba   *have mercy Father*
Shwele Nkosi yami   *have mercy My Lord*
children send you
to and fro
the world eats grass Baba
people chew sorghum beer
you're lying on the ground
no pocket money
no bread
brown musk overall
bloodstained
danger races outdoors
Shwele Baba
Shwele Nkosi yami
Hail the King
Hail our great
Nomandumbuluzane   *god/goddess, originator of life*

Nonhlanhla

Nonhlanhla is gone
tears pearls laughter
dreads survey my toes
touch of anguish
pat my mind
the target is found
Nonhlanhla is gone

They nailed her
pink nails oozing
they dragged her
reshuffled her
off the ground
pinned her tongue
hanging loose
blood pool flooded
to dry up heavens
Nonhlanhla is gone
staring
into the dark
tired of Nkosi yami   *my Lord*
go away
biting my lips
my dark room walls
caressing the belt
to end the beginning
of a far away song

In my mind
Zion bells ring
bayavuya   *they are happy*
umoya wami uyakhathazeka   *my soul gets troubled*
voices crying

in the dark
darkness
swallows the light
my heart
has stopped beating
no mercy in Zion
Nonhlanhla is gone

Mr Brown

Brown
white
behind my unit
I see you
today and everyday
painting
in weird colours

Mr Brown
drowning in my soup
playing hide and seek
with the spider man
you are his bread
for lunch
stop your
jumble sale
games
Mr Brown

Push aside squeaky

Push aside squeaky
sky scrubbed
to the blue
door to door
volle homey hi   *many homeys here*
in chaff pozies   *in illicit hiding-places*
them no good never buy
mashakara is hulle mos   *they are a gang*
pounding hearts knock
search
suna papa nana   *kiss daddy baby*
mochochonono drive   *streamline*
van corner
bafedile   *they are finished*
binne kasie   *in the location*
in eight kant
cancer bantwana   *White City babes*
drum ten distribute   *rural zulu distribute*
bullet holes in their pockets
ba tsokotsa diketlele   *they rinse kettles*
dikgogedi di kolobetsa matjhaba *attractive things baptise nations*
goody goody boys
scaffolding
bunch to bunch
in cook dladlas   *in shebeens*
push aside squeaky
pidi pidi   *the duck*
ha ena meno   *has no teeth*

Thokozani

Open doors wide
for fresh air
se isi pelo magoletsa   *don't let your emotions rise*
Phefeni knows Mmabatho
Mofolo bare ke mmabona   *Mofolo they say is their mother*
hayani she stays   *home*
here she packs
there she goes
banthati ba kana ka bantlhoi *as many love me as hate me*
the villagers
and neighbours chuck me
no water to drink
no food to eat
shelter see to finish
no sunshine for me
God gives
God takes
He takes all
for us who care
no beards to caress
nor lamb to lullaby
countless souls hate her
a pound of flesh suffers
no peace of mind
bricks break
thoughts free
tshingandededze   *veins keep me moving*
ba ithobaletseng   *those who are peacefully asleep/dead*
she kneels down
hand in hand
ntsu snuff
Thokozani
she cried

re utliwe phuthuloha   *we heard your cries   be comforted*
o seke wa tshwenyeha   *do not be bothered/troubled*
voices cry deeper
in black berry night
pillow rocks for
vivid apparition
white cloth
red beads
se ise pelo magoletsa   *don't let your emotions rise*
Thokozani

Work shire

Kana ka sega phefo
ka ralla dinaga
ka rakana le monna
are Yorkshire
England kwa moroba
tiro emo batla mabogo
ka e bona
ka e tshwantshanya
le small heaven
naare yena ke Yorkshire
tlogela botsoropa wena
bothakga gabo rekwe
banna ba kwa Tsetse Tsitsi
mesong ba sadisa dikobo
kwa Jo'burg
ba bolawa ke more kom

Work shire

I sliced the wind
I traversed many lands
I met a man
who said Yorkshire England
is a place of leisure
and they need hands to work
I went there I saw
it was just like
a small heaven
this Yorkshire
I said let me not
hold myself back with excuses
talent cannot be bought
mornings
Tsetse Tsitsi men bid their blankets goodbye
They go to Joburg
where 'come tomorrow'
kills them

Tlong beso

Paaha
tlong beso
paaha
tlong beso
ke nako ya ho hlaola
ke nako ya kotulo
tlong re buisaneng
tlong ka kutlwano
paaha
tlong beso
paaha
tlong beso
selemo se thwasitse
mabele a hodile
na le utlwile na
taba ketse monate
paaha
tlong beso
paaha
tlong beso

Come my people

Paaha
come people
paaha
come my people
it is time to weed
it is time to harvest
come let us talk
come in peace
paaha
come people
paaha
come my people
the summer has broken
the grain has grown
have you heard
the good news
paaha
come people
paaha
come my people

Hoshe ngwana

Hoshe ngwana
gata o gatoge
melodi kafa le fa
ngwana dikoti marameng
pososelo eka naledi
sefahleho sone
botjhitja bo kgatlang mahlo
re bone mesebetsi ya hao
naheng mona
ba reng
o sekobo
ke baikaketsi
ba lese ba iphore jaalo
shine bright sunbeam
hoha
kana wena o motswa mantlha
gata o gatoge thope
shine bright sunbeam
hoshe thope
hoha
moo o fetileng
ho sala dinaledi
ho ha
thebetha Mohlakwana
thebetha Mofokeng
re bone mesebetsi ya hao
digaboi di tseleng jwale
raak hulle dizzy ousie
slaat hulle giddy poppy
ba fehlile jwale
ba ho bapallang sax

Hey babe

Hey baby
walk with a strut
                 draw all the whistles
           with the dimples in your cheeks
                 smile like you're a star
as for your face
its roundness pleases the eye
here in the country
those who say
you are ugly
they lie to themselves
let them fool themselves
shine bright sunbeam
wow
          you're the best
walk with a strut girl
you are number one
hey girl
ho ha
shine bright sunbeam
                 when you walk past
wow
stars are left behind
pride yourself Mohlakwana
pride yourself Mofokeng
make them dizzy sister
hit them giddy doll
they have arrived now
those who play sax for you

Tlopo kgubedu

Bonang wee
bonang yoo
lapeng la heso
ho tsikitsano ya meno
basadi ba kgelella dikeledi
bosiu le motsehare
tlopo kgubedu
kgoho e ntsho e kene
lapeng la heso
ngwana mme ntate
e qadile ka ntja ka ntle
a kobotile ho fihla leseeng
bonang wee
bonang yoo
re tla bona re entse
jwang na
thepa e ile yohle
re fuma keledi tsa
mosadi ka tlung
mme wee ese ele pina

Red helmet

oh look
oh see
at my house
                there's a gnashing of teeth
women's tears gather
night and day
                a black fowl
                has entered my house
child mother father
it started with the dog outside
it has now reached the baby
oh look
oh see
how will we get
through this
our possessions are all gone
we wipe the tears
                of the woman of the house
'oh mother' is now the song

Rope sa motswetse

Basadi matlung
banna ntle
ho qaaka mona
banna akgelang
pelo ya morena
melamu le se e lebale
phala di be ho lona
ho qaaka mona
mosadi a tswa a kgenne
a jele sekaja
fuba di le moyeng
mose o kuketswe dinokeng
monna qosheletsaneng
tedu hase tsa botsofe
tedu ke tsa lekaota
mosadi wa chobolo
o lebisitse bohale lekaoteng
la hloka ho tsotella
la tswela pele le peipi
phate tsa lahleha motseng
tjhaba sa hloka kgotso
fanang beso
fanang ka tlotla
fanang ka kgotso
fanang ka rope sa motswetse
le ahe kgotso motseng
Morena hlwella dithaba
o kope kgotso ho ramasedi
a ho sedimosetse
rapedisa pula Morena
kgomo tsa ntate
di tshwerwe ke lenyora
baahisane haba mahlong

Thigh of the new mother

Women indoors
men outdoors
there is a problem here
                              men throw out
the heart of the king
do not forget your fighting-sticks
                    keep your whistles with you
there is a problem here
a woman came out angry
in full flight
                    chest puffed out up in the air
dress hitched up to the hip-bone
man run and hide (deep in the undergrowth)
beard belongs to the lone warrior
the woman who is a shrew
pointed her sharpness at the young strong warrior
he paid no attention
he just continued smoking his pipe
blankets got lost in the neighbourhood
the nation was without peace
                              give us peace
                              give us respect
give of peace
give of the thigh of the new mother
build peace in the neighbourhood
king climb the mountains
ask for peace from the almighty
may he bless you
pray for rain king
my father's cattle
they are thirsty
neighbours do not look one another in the eye
they have had fried for them

ba hadiketswe
dithose melomong
metsi ha hosa kgellanwa
tsena ditaba di mahlong

seeds in the eyes
we no longer draw water for one another
these matters are in the eye

Ribbon hands

Ribbon hands
mama's little darling
matsoho ke dikgabisa
o botswa ho re ha ho le tjena
ya boi a tjhetjhe
nkane e bonala phatleng
bana ke dikgutsana
mambo a sa ja abele
hoseng oya mosebetsing
seeta sea hatwa hle
manala ha o hloke pente
makgowa a mo tseba e le
Mrs so and so
kajeno nyalo e fedile
a dula marao jarateng
tsa boMastens
roll on
mabhobhodlwane
ke ntlentletse
ho aparwa di miniskirt
ntata ke enwa
hosasa ke yaane

Ribbon hands

Ribbon hands
mama's little darling
hands are decorations
she is so lazy
cowards should keep away
stubbornness is seen on the forehead
children are orphans
while the mother still eats sorghum
in the morning she goes to work
oh how the shoe gets stepped on
the nails lack for no paint
whites know her as
Mrs so and so
today her marriage is finished
she plonks her buttocks
in the yards
of landladies
roll on
young females
are in over-abundance
they wear mini-skirts
now the problem is this one
tomorrow it is that one

Tributes for Isabella
(first published in Botsotso 13)

Stomach ulcer complications
Isabella Motadinyane (1963-2003)
Ike Mboneni Muila

on the day i received sad news of her sudden death in a clinic/hospital orange farm i was shattered i felt stomach butterflies running all over the show then i felt something rising towards my throat and there i was speechless and howling like a dog without its bone. isabella motadinyane was born on the 17th feb. 1963 mofolo central and passed away suffering from a death of speech in a hospital/clinic orange farm on the 19th jan. 2003. she wrote a poem that gave birth to botsotso publishers and botsotso poetry performers as botsotso jesters.

i met isabella while a stage manager in a workshopped play about life in theatre...pimville of the early sixties...gangsterism, music and social politics of that time even the tsotsitaal lingo used at that particular times under the title skom short for skomplaas that is emzini...at home...during tea time and lunch time we would be discussing creative writing that is poetry and state drama performance complementing each other she became my soulmate and told me to throw away my walking stick which i used to keep my body upright while struggling with the force of gravity since my permanent brain fracture blow i suffered in 91 jeppe street jozi, i wrote her a poem...my better half...

she also told me of her sad story. she told me she won't live long because of her stomach ulcer complication. she told me her mother took her to a family planning clinic for sterile and birth control while she was a young school kid for fear of unwanted pregnancy she told me her tubes got blocked and that led to her life threatening situation... stomach sore pains which would finally take her life.

to me she was such a strong sister soldier and fighter who does not easily bow down to minor pains then she would curl up in bed next to me giving me squeaky sound of ehchu...farting and laughing hysterical when i ask her why was that she would tell me the pain is gone out with the fart we would both laugh hysterical...while she continues to fart i would hold her kiss her and then ask her what she would love to drink before and after meal as a wash down she would tell me she is tired of drinking white water that is milk sugar and hot water as her one and only tea she would love to drink beer and be merry waya waya to entertain the mass of poetry lovers with a beer in a hand drinking like nobody's business and with our own creative writing coming home with raving reviews.

i could now remember vividly she wrote sink a shaft before a beer bottle while we were rehearsing poetry and spontaneously collectively creating and recreating folk songs that would go along with the poetry in grahamstown poetry festival performance...since 1993 to 98 after an evening performance we would go to the nearest wimpy bar or favourite pub to rewind chanting poetry brain-storming and discussing possible channels for our creative effort and going to sleep after hours sure no matter how much drunk we could be that we wake up on time to take a shower or a warm bath.during our collective effort she would come up with melody and then we would sit down jointly work on the lyrics and finally write down the folk songs for example vulani song, bonang wee, bantwana song written and recorded in the 1998 performance poetry festival video grahamstown with isabella in rhodes university video title jikeleza train...

isabella motadinyane was a born genius she went as far as grade 5 at school...highly spiritual person chosen by her ancestors to serve them as a sangoma to be... if you argue or disagree without any valid reasonable point ... uyadoya you fail dismal she would put you to shame and prove you wrong on the spot and make you feel stupid she does not care whether you are white or black makhulu baas or top shayela...academic bra at school she memorized a narrative from the unknown author "the extract from the dangerous ground" which could beautifully chant word for word with such a marvellous understanding to me. she was extraordinary singer, dancer, poet, actress, performer, a unique soulmate and we used to influence each other in one way or the other at times we could stay away from drinking for six to seven weeks period during that time facing the harshness of life reality...

sober-minded in pains she would come to me and say that there is something which is running from her stomach to her throat and choking her making it difficult for her to breathe...and you could see her hopeless pale face and that she is in a pensive mood and losing weight and then she would go on for weeks praying and taking instructions from her ancestors consulting with christian prophets sangomas friends for advice then slowly she would regain her weight and her face looking brighter she would come up with those ehchu...ehchu sound farting and we would both laugh hysterical that the pain is gone out with the fart then we would resume our eat and drinking spree when she is good and ready in her pretty mood with her strong spiritual belief she would say to me amongst her ancestors she is guided by three outstanding characters, a christian prophet, a sangoma and an aggressive dumb founded instructor who facilitates messages amongst christian prophets and sangomas...the dumb founded character usually visit her when she is on a beer drinking spree and also come in on special visit or a call to deliver and facilitate an assignment amongst people she used to work with practice or help or assist she could not charge on her own accord her patients she could only go along with what they give her as long as at the end of the day she could afford a beer to console herself and rejoice. and that used to make me feel sad and disoriented because even people in the arts in the creative writing and poetry performances people just want to be entertained mahala free bees they just don't feel like paying or buying products of the arts they don't care what you eat at the end of the day or how you make a living – they just don't have respect for our creative efforts as artist and that is why we perish in vain and so poor wihout anyone who cares a damn at the end of the day jikelele...

For Isabella
Allan Kolski Horwitz

We came in the rain
to your mother's house
we found you on your back
in a small coffin
behind a thin curtain

three old women on a mattress
wrapped in black cloth and towels
men in the yard skinning a cow
entrails piled in a heap
like your poems stacked in books or on the stages
where you rode Coltrane's sunship
tight jeaned botsotsos
survivors
of the land of plenty
climbing aboard to join the refrain

the cow peers through the window
we drink tea, eat biscuits
the body of your work
jiving in our memories

before death came
your friend tells us
your tongue swelled
you couldn't eat
couldn't give voice
even for Nonhlanhla who was attacked
breaking your heart with her spilt pearls

now in praise we sing to you
to the taxi topsy turvy
you caught at the corner of kerk and nugget

to the sweet shafts you sank
to the back pockets that need to be mended
to the three old women
on the mattress

we drink tea in the rain:
hamba kahle, botsotso sister

Bella: Kosesishiyile u-Isabella Motadinyane
Siphiwe ka Ngwenya

Qhawekazi lakwaMotadinyane
Amany'amagam'ayoshabalala
kodw'elakho liyohlala ngunaphakade
ekujuleni kwemicabango yethu
wena gugu lamagugu ngobugagu bakho

izwi lakho eliwumzwilili we-Blues
liyohlala lintyiloza ezindlebeni zami
lingithi gidi isibindi emphefumulweni wami
ngiswele amagam'aqotho najulil'awokuthopha
kawufanga ulele ngoba igama lakho kalipheli
ezindebeni zethu

uma ngicabanga ngawe gagu le-Botsotso
kuhlengezel'umvimbi wezinyembezi
uwelele kwelabaphansi
 uwelele kwelikaMvelinqangi
siyohlala sikukhumbuuulaaa! Thokoza!

Bella

To Isabella Motadinyane who has passed on
Siphiwe ka Ngwenya

Heroine of the Motadinyanes
other names fade away
but yours will stay forever
deep in the depth of our thoughts
you favourite of favourites with your golden voice

Your sweet bluesy voice
will echo harmoniously like a bird in my ears
giving me strength in my soul
i yearn for righteous and deep words of exaltation
you are not dead, but are asleep
your name shall never slip away from our lips

when i think of you
a torrential rain of tears flows
you have crossed over to ancestral land
the land of Mvelinqangi
we shall always remember you! Thokoza!

My better half
Ike Mboneni Muila

This poem used to be sung by Isabella as a jazz & blues song

Love nest well
in hard times
together
in difficulties
cooldrinks
both of us
down the bottom
of hardship
hard times
mafanya life...

money here money there
in good times
buy a cooldrink
joburg our home
our stable
window pane
drink it cool

my better half
we built a home
on top of a rock
our joburg home

we had hard times
in difficulties together
come rain come
though thunderstorms
my better half
thou shall never
wither

Printed in the United States
By Bookmasters